# UNDERSTANDING NATURAL DISASTERS

# Volcanoes, Earthquakes, & Tsunamis

## Books in this series:

Firestorms & Wildfires

Floods & Mudslides

Thunderstorms & Blizzards

Typhoons & Hurricanes

Volcanoes, Earthquakes, & Tsunamis

**UNDERSTANDING NATURAL DISASTERS**

# Volcanoes, Earthquakes, & Tsunamis

Chance Parker

**Understanding Natural Disasters**
**Volcanoes, Earthquakes, & Tsunamis**

Copyright © 2016 by Village Earth Press, a division of Harding House Publishing. All rights reserved. No part of this publication may be reproduced or transmitted in any form or by any means, electronic or mechanical, including photocopying, recording, taping, or any information storage and retrieval system, without permission from the publisher.

Village Earth Press
Vestal, New York 13850
www.villageearthpress.com

First Printing
9 8 7 6 5 4 3 2 1

Series ISBN (paperback): 978-1-62524-447-5
ISBN (paperback): 978-1-62524-434-5
ebook ISBN: 978-1-62524-120-7
   Library of Congress Control Number: 2014934545

Author: Parker, Chance.

# Contents:

| | |
|---|---|
| Volcanoes, Earthquakes, and Tsunamis | 7 |
| Staying Safe | 40 |
| Find Out More | 43 |
| Glossary Words | 45 |
| Index | 47 |
| About the Author & Picture Credits | 48 |

Planet Earth is our home. It gives us life. But our planet can also be dangerous! It can shake up people and their homes. When our planet does that, we call it a natural disaster. The Earth doesn't mean to hurt us, of course. It's just doing what comes naturally.

Volcanoes, earthquakes, and tsunamis are all natural disasters. They are big and exciting—but sometimes they smash homes and towns and cities.

A disaster is something bad that upsets our lives.

A volcano is a mountain that opens down into the liquid rock that's inside the Earth. The mountain was made when the liquid rock pushed its way out.

The liquid rock is called magma when it's inside the Earth—but when it pushes its way outside, it is called lava. It is very, very hot!

A liquid is anything that's runny. Water, milk, and orange juice are all liquids. Magma is a very, very thick liquid!

Some volcano mountains have lava that still shoots out their tops.

Other volcanoes have gone to sleep.

Sometimes sleeping volcanoes wake up!

An earthquake is when the Earth's crust shakes. Sometimes it cracks open. When that happens, houses and other buildings shake too.

During an earthquake, a house might shake so much that things fall off the shelves and break.

The crust of something is the outer layer. The crust of a loaf of bread is the tough, brown part on the outside, and the Earth's crust is its hard outer layer.

Sometimes an earthquake makes cracks across roads.

Sometimes during a bad earthquake, walls and roofs break. Sometimes buildings fall down!

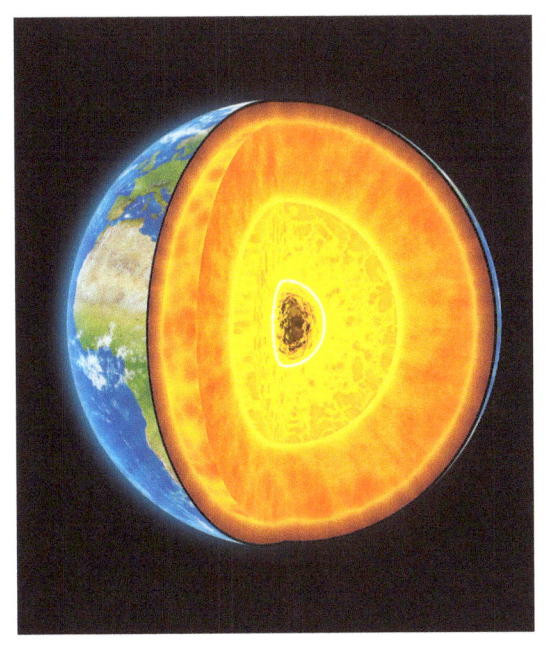

All this happens when something inside the Earth moves. The movement on the inside is what shakes up the Earth's crust. If you could crack the Earth open and look inside, you'd see something like this. There's a lot going on inside our planet!

Volcanoes and earthquakes happen because of movement going on inside the Earth. And volcanoes and earthquakes can make another kind of natural disaster happen. They can cause tsunamis. Tsunamis are made when earthquakes or volcanoes happen under or near the ocean.

A tsunami is an enormous wave.

When a tsunami hits the shore, it can wash away houses and cars.

It can knock down buildings. It leaves behind a big mess!

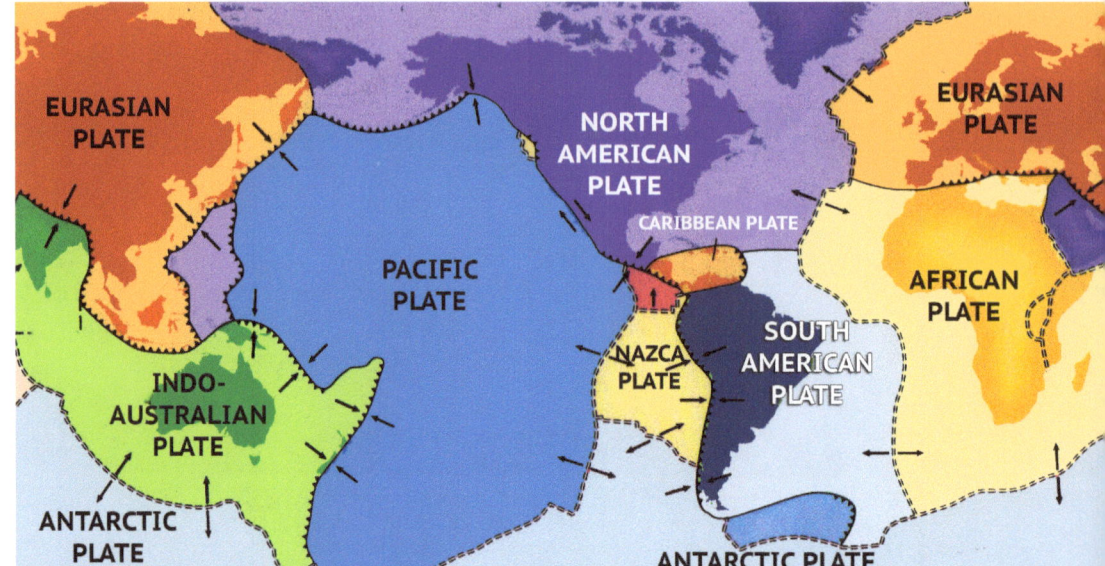

Volanoes, earth-quakes, and tsunamis all happen because of movement inside the Earth. They happen because our planet is made of enormous slabs of rock. These huge layers of rock are called "tectonic plates." The Earth has eight big plates and lots of smaller ones. This map shows the big plates and a couple of the smaller ones.

The plates are like the skin of the planet. They are floating on a thick layer of magma. Because they are floating, they move around the planet.

Do you remember what magma is? It's rock that's so hot that it's turned into a very thick liquid.

You can't see the plates move. They move very slowly. But when they bump into each other, they push on each other.

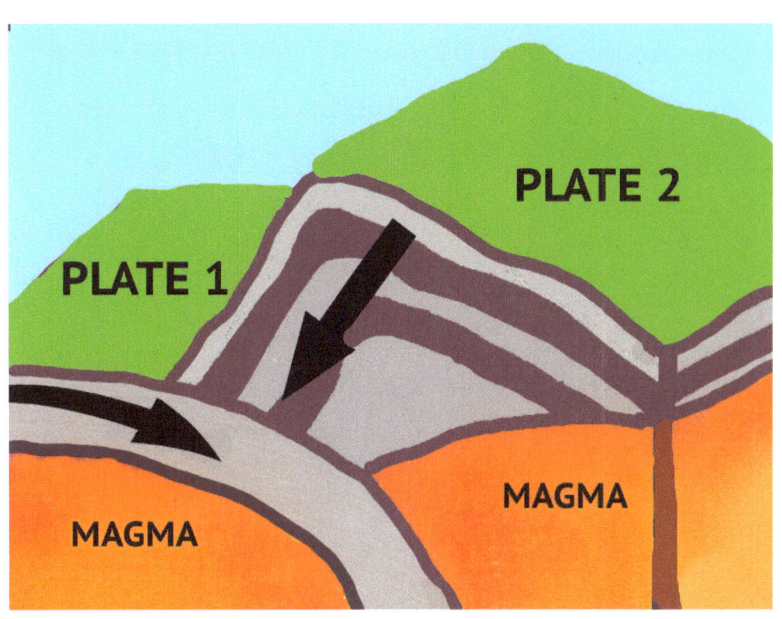

Imagine if you were pushing on both ends of a stick. The stick would start to bend. Sooner or later, the stick would break. That's a little like what happens with the Earth's plates. When they push on each other, they create pressure.

Pressure is what happens when you press very hard on something.

All that pressure has to go somewhere! When the pressure is great enough, the crust is forced to break. When the break occurs, the pressure's energy moves through the Earth in waves. Those waves are what cause earthquakes. The waves move out from the center point where the pressure broke the crust. That point is called the epicenter.

Energy is what makes things move. It's what gives power to things (and people).

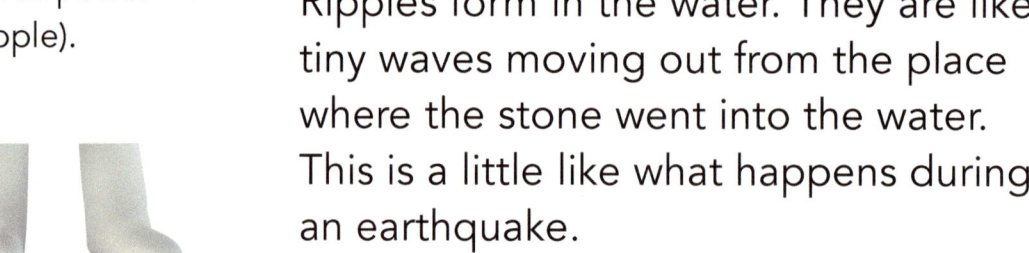

This time imagine that you're throwing a stone into a lake. What happens? Ripples form in the water. They are like tiny waves moving out from the place where the stone went into the water. This is a little like what happens during an earthquake.

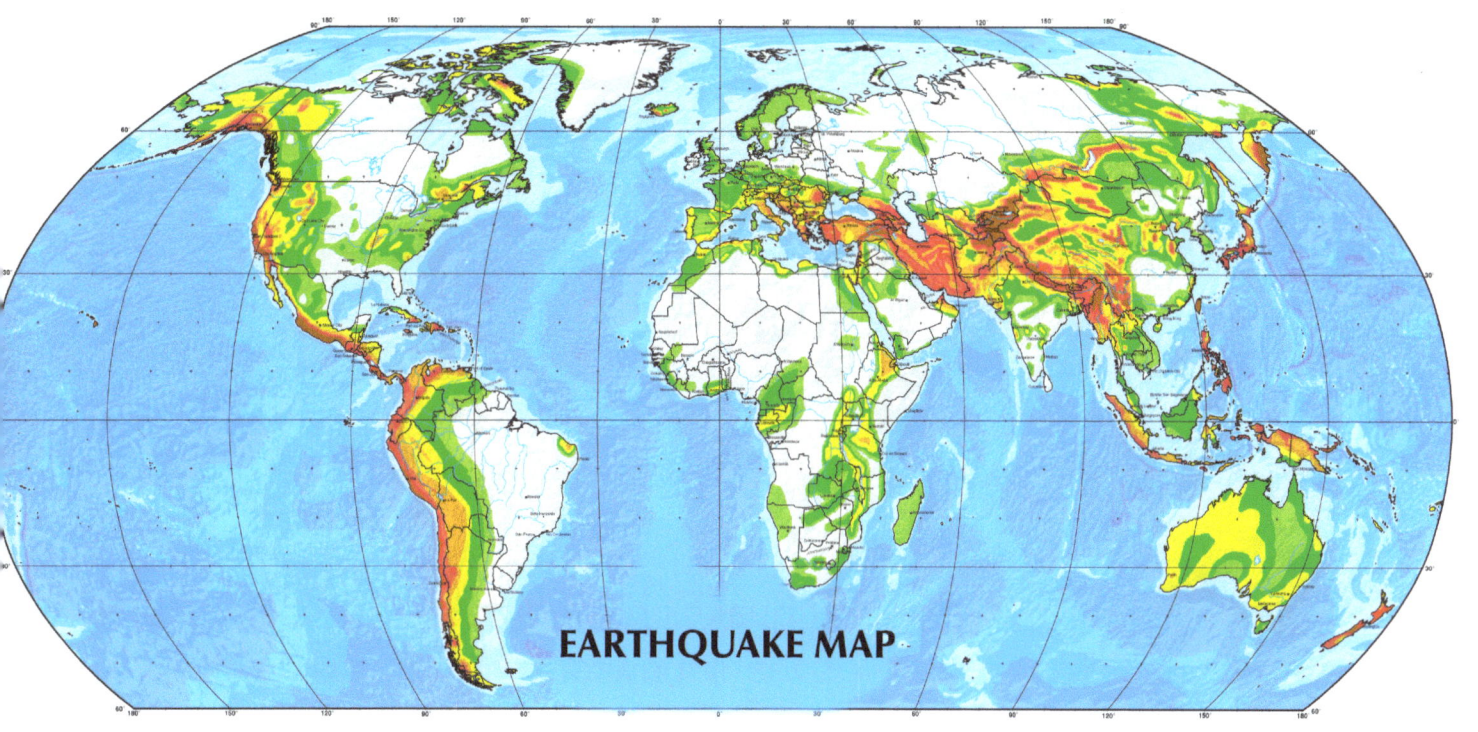

EARTHQUAKE MAP

Most earthquakes happen along the edges of the Earth's tectonic plates. This is why earthquakes usually only happen in certain parts of the world. This map shows where earthquakes are most likely to happen. The areas that are red are where most earthquakes take place. The parts of the map that are white have very few if any earthquakes.

Scientists say they can measure about 500,000 earthquakes every year. Only 100,000 can be felt, though. And only about 100 hurt buildings and roads.

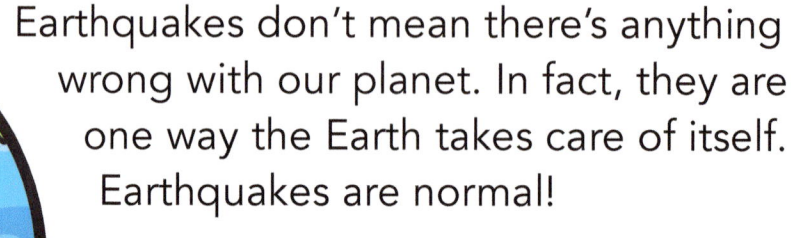

Earthquakes don't mean there's anything wrong with our planet. In fact, they are one way the Earth takes care of itself. Earthquakes are normal!

When earthquakes push on the Earth's crust, over millions of years they form mountains. Without mountains, the Earth's weather would change.

When wind blows against mountains, the air is forced to rise. This makes the air colder. As it gets colder, it makes clouds—and those clouds drop rain on the Earth. The Earth needs rain!

Without the mountains made by earthquakes, rivers wouldn't run to the sea. Our planet would not look the same.

Earthquakes also help to keep our planet the right temperature. They release heat from the Earth's core, which scientists think is why our planet has air and water. Life on Earth would be very different if there were no earthquakes!

When scientists study earthquakes, they get clues about the inside of the Earth. Earthquakes teach us more about our planet.

Scientists are people who try to find the answers to questions about the world around them. You can be a scientist right now!

Earthquakes and volcanoes are linked together. Earthquakes often happen before a volcano is born. Like earthquakes, most volcanoes form along the edges of Earth's tectonic plates. When the plates shift during an earthquake, they jostle the magma that lies beneath the Earth's crust. The magma starts moving. It melts more rock. As the magma builds up, it pushes on the Earth's crust. If the pressure becomes great enough, it will force a hole in the crust. Then the magma squirts through this hole. It shoots up into the air. Now it is called lava. The lava builds up in a cone-shaped mountain. It cools and becomes solid again.

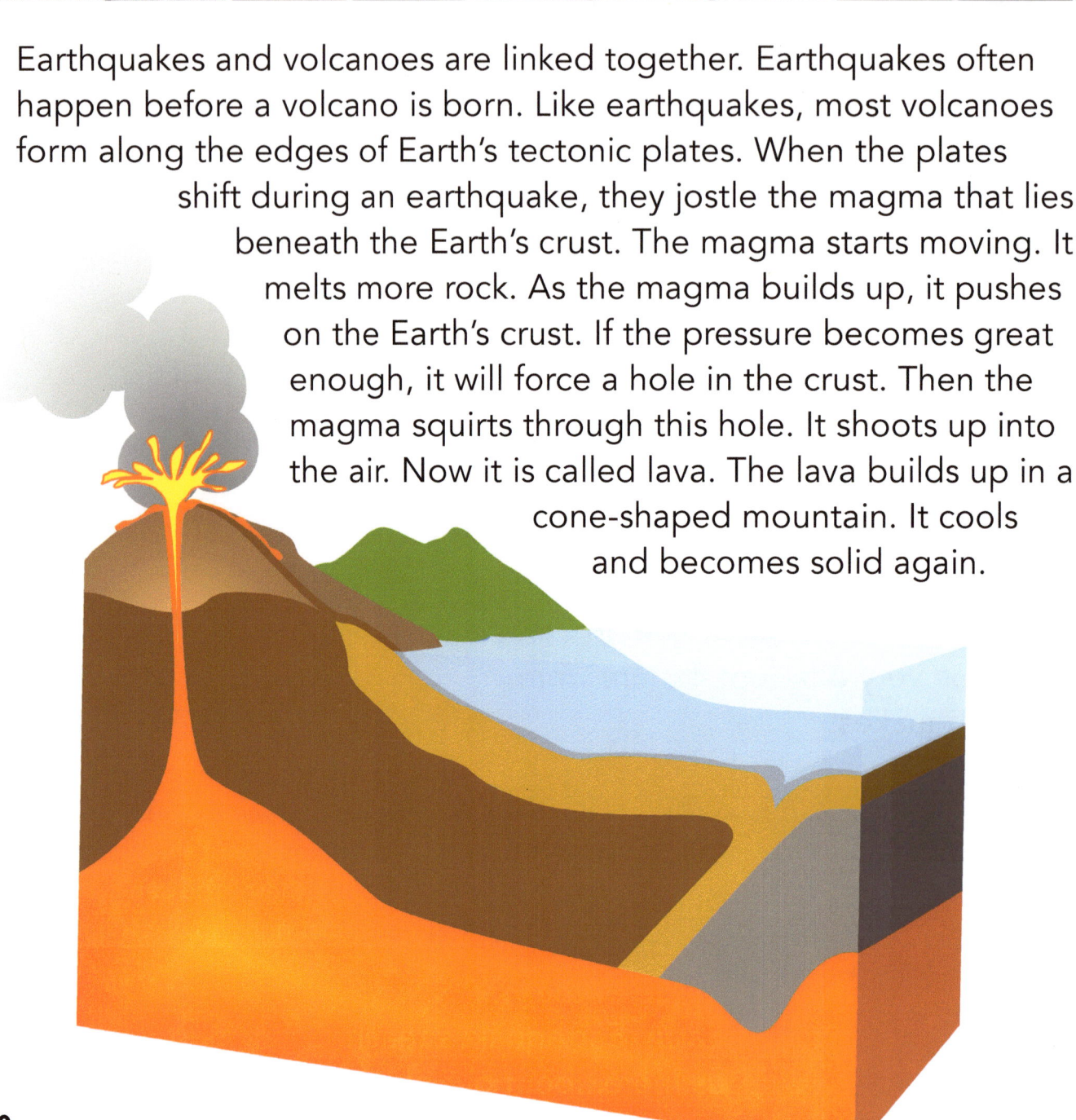

As more lava flows from the top of the volcano, the mountain of lava gets bigger and bigger.

Sometimes volcanoes can cause earthquakes. Magma puts pressure on the Earth's crust. It pushes hard against it until it cracks. Each time it cracks, an earthquake happens. Most of these earthquakes are too small to feel, though.

Lava isn't the only thing that shoots out of the top of a volcano. Ash also comes out of a volcano. The ash is made of very tiny, sharp pieces of rock.

The ash looks a big dark cloud. The wind can blow the ash away from the volcano. It can be so thick that it makes daytime seem like night, so that people can't see where they are going. It can land on people's homes. It can even knock down buildings and power lines.

But ash is also good for soil. It adds nutrients that help plants grow. The land around volcanoes is often good farmland.

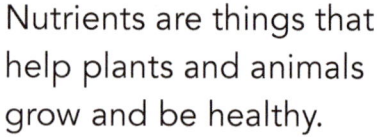

Nutrients are things that help plants and animals grow and be healthy.

Like earthquakes, volcanoes are good for our planet. They're another way of letting off heat from the Earth's hot core. They make mountains and islands.

Over millions of years, the gases that come out of volcanoes are what made our atmosphere. Without the atmosphere, we wouldn't be able to breathe. The sun's heat would burn us to a crisp. There would be no life on Earth!

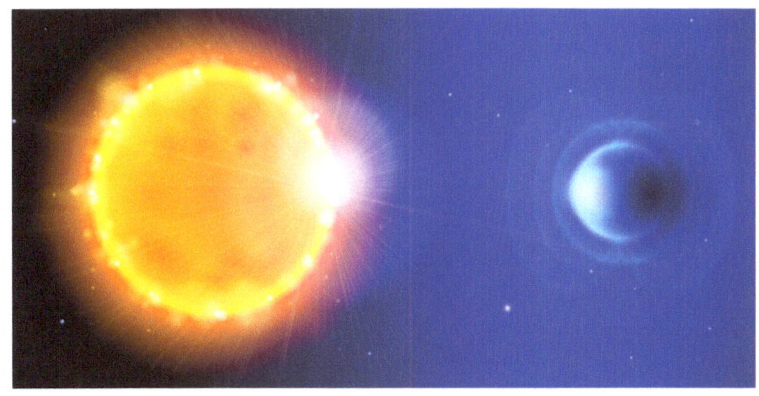

The atmosphere is the layer of air that surrounds the Earth.

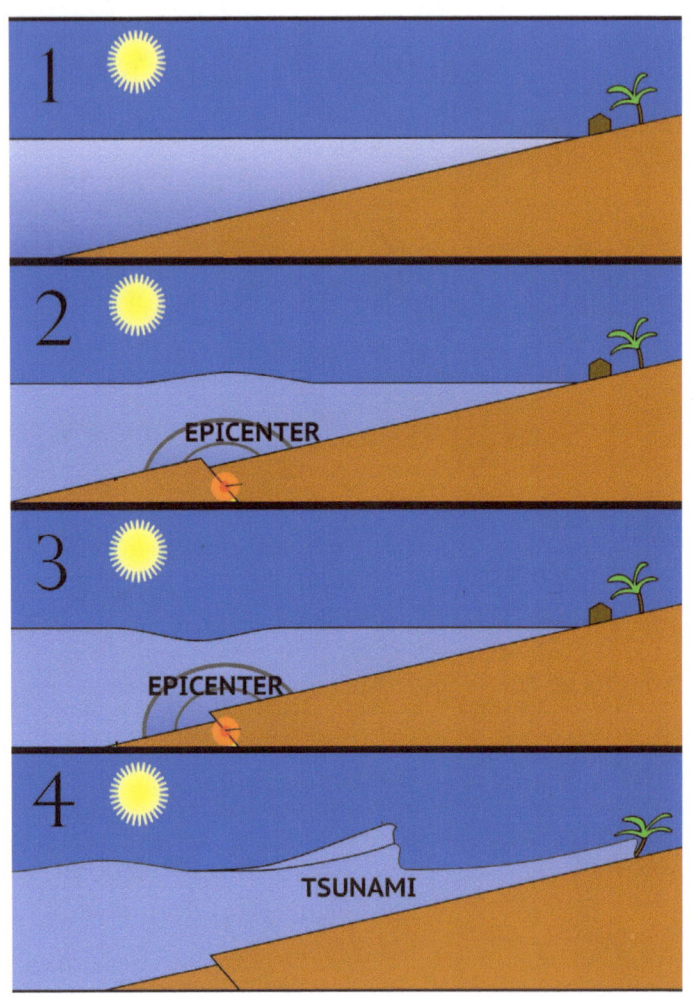

Both volcanoes and earthquakes can make tsunamis. This picture shows what happens when an earthquake happens under the ocean. An earthquake or a volcano beneath the ocean will move the ocean floor. It's a little like when you're in the bathtub and you move your legs back and forth. The movement of your legs makes the water slosh back and forth. An earthquake or a volcano under the ocean makes a lot of water slosh up onto the land.

The water makes a huge wave. The wave can travel a long way from the earthquake or volcano. It is like a wall of water. It can be 100 feet tall! That's longer than a basketball court.

When the wave hits the land, it crashes into buildings and trees. It leaves behind big floods. Cars and buses and people's homes may all float away.

A forge is a very hot place where metal can be melted and made into tools and weapons.

Today we understand a lot more about what makes earthquakes, volcanoes, and tsunamis. Long ago, people didn't know what made these huge disasters. Sometimes they blamed gods for making them happen. The word "volcano" comes from the name of one of these gods—Vulcan. Vulcan was the god of fire. Long ago, the people who lived in what is today the country of Italy believed in Vulcan. They thought he lived deep beneath a volcano called Mount Etna. There he made his weapons in his fiery forge.

Mount Etna is still an active volcano. It still shoots out lava and fire!

Erupt is the word for what volcanoes do when they shoot out lava.

Another famous volcano from history is Mount Vesuvius. It was also in Italy. Nearly 2,000 years ago, Mount Vesuvius erupted. The city of Pompeii was completely buried in ash. For hundreds of years the city was lost.

Then its ruins were discovered. They were hidden beneath the ash. Now people can explore the old, old city. They can see what life was like for the people who lived there.

The worst earthquake happened almost 500 years ago in a place called Shaanxi in China. It killed 830,000 people. No other earthquake has been as bad. Then, almost 300 years ago, a huge earthquake hit the city of Lisbon in Portugal. This earthquake also caused a tsunami. Fires broke out after the earthquake. In the end, the city was almost completely destroyed.

Earthquakes often cause fires. They can tip over stoves and bring down power lines. They can also break pipes that carry gas. A little more than 100 years ago, an earthquake shook the city of San Francisco. The earthquake caused a huge fire that swept through the city.

About 2,500 years ago, armies were invading Greece when an enormous wave arose in the sea and pushed them back. The people of Greece thanked the god Poseidon for protecting them. They believed that Poseidon drove his horses to form the enormous wave. Scientists today believe that it was actually a tsunami that pushed away Greece's enemies.

Japan has always had a lot of tsunamis. Four hundred years ago, a mysterious tsunami flooded several villages in Japan. The waves seemed to come out of nowhere, waking up the villagers in the middle of the night. The Japanese were already used to tsunamis, but they knew that an earthquake needed to come first, before the huge waves. This time, no one had felt the earth shake. They didn't understand where the waves had come from.

Scientists today found the answer! They learned that an enormous earthquake took place about the same time 5,000 miles away in northwestern North American, in what is today part of Canada and the United States. That earthquake sent a tsunami all the way across the Pacific Ocean!

Earthquakes have happened ever since the Earth was born. They are still happening today. In 2005, a big quake hit a place called Kashmir in the Asian country of Pakistan. The homes, schools, and other buildings there were not built to stand up during an earthquake. Many people were trapped inside the buildings that fell down.

It cost millions of dollars to build back all the buildings that fell down. In the meantime, many families had to live in tents, like the children shown in this picture.

In 2010, a big earthquake shook Haiti, an island country in the Caribbean Ocean. The first big quake was followed by more than 50 smaller quakes in the days that followed. Thousands of people died. About 250,000 homes fell down.

Almost 2 million people were left without any place to live. Many families had to live in tents made out of sheets of plastic.

Like earthquakes, volcanoes have always been a part of what the Earth does naturally. They continue to happen, and they always will! About 35 years ago, a volcano in the United States called Mount St. Helens erupted. The volcano had been asleep for more than a hundred years. No magma pushed up inside it during all that time. No lava flowed out of its top. Then in 1980, an earthquake woke up the volcano! When it did, the volcano killed people and smashed houses. It broke bridges, railways, and roads. It was a big disaster!

Another volcano called Mount Merapi has been awake for almost 500 years. The mountain is on the line between two Asian countries, Java and Indonesia. Its name means "Fire Mountain" in the language of the people who live there.

Mount Merapi has smoke coming out of its top almost every day of the year. In 2010, the government of Indonesia warned the people who lived near the volcano to get out. Scientists knew that the volcano was getting ready to blow its top in a big way! Earthquakes shook the land. Lava and ash blew out from the top of the volcano. There was so much ash in the air that airplanes could not fly near there for days afterward. This picture was taken from a satellite far, far above the Earth on the day that the volcano erupted. You can see how big the cloud of ash was that rose out of the mountain!

A satellite is like a small space ship without any people on it. It circles the Earth, sending back photographs and other information to scientists on Earth.

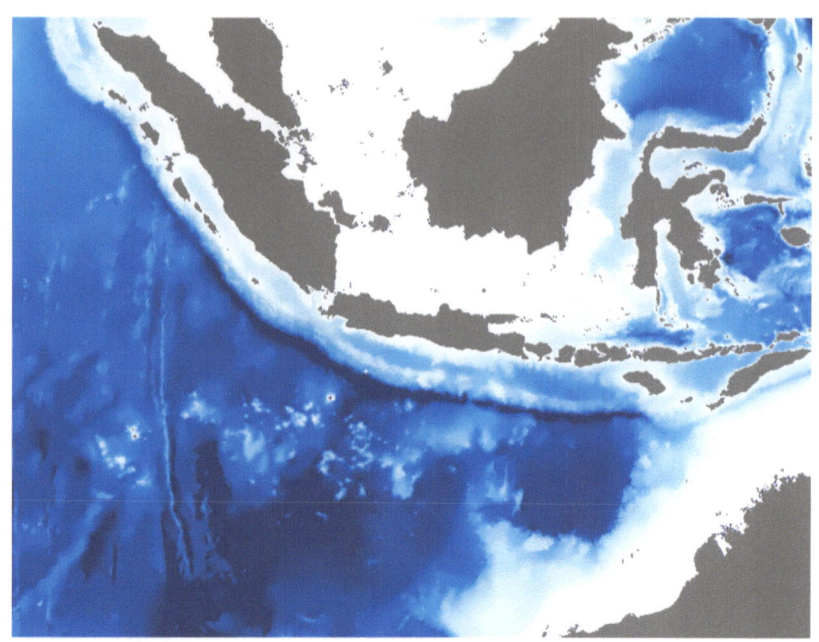

On December 26, 2004, a very big earthquake shook the floor of the Indian Ocean and made a huge tsunami. The tsunami hit twelve countries, including India, Thailand, and Malaysia. This photograph of the tsunami waves was taken from a satellite high in space. About 230,000 people died because of the tsunami, and many, many more lost their homes.

The waves traveled all the way around the Earth, to northeastern North America and the coast of South America. By the time they reached the other side of the world, they were much smaller, though.

The coast is where land and water meet.

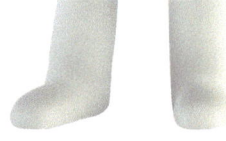

The fourth-largest earthquake that we know about shook Japan on March 11, 2011. Japan was ready for earthquakes, and the earthquake itself didn't hurt the country too much. But it created a big, big tsunami that took some people by surprise. It washed over towns and cities along Japan's coast. This picture shows a building that the tsunami knocked down. All that's left are bricks!

There's nothing we can do to keep earthquakes, volcanoes, and tsunamis from happening. They're just part of how the Earth works. But scientists have learned how to tell when our planet is getting ready to shake or erupt. The Earth gives off warning signs ahead of time. Scientists watch closely for these signs. When they can tell that an earthquake, volcano, or tsunami is about to happen, they warn people. Then people can go somewhere safe. This little girl and her family left their home before Mount Merapi erupted in 2010. The government gave her and others like her a safe place to camp. They also gave them food.

Engineers are also learning to make buildings and roads so that they don't fall down so easily during an earthquake. They are making buildings and roads that move with the Earth instead of breaking and falling apart. This means that people are safer if an earthquake happens. This skyscraper in San Francisco is specially made so that it won't fall down the next time an earthquake hits the city!

An earthquake in the South American country of Chile knocked down an old church. This church was built in its place. It is made so that earthquakes won't hurt it. When a big earthquake hit Chile in 2010, the only damage to the church was a few broken windows!

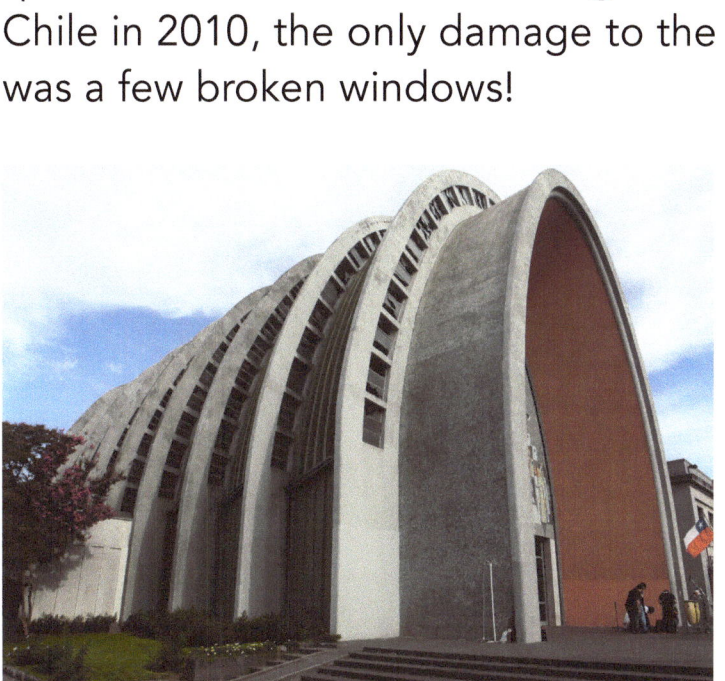

Engineers are people who plan, build, and take care of buildings, bridges, and roads.

# Staying Safe!

More than a million earthquakes shake up the Earth each year! Some of them go along with volcanoes. A few of them cause tsunamis. These natural disasters can be pretty scary—but there are things you can do to stay safe.

## EARTHQUAKES

If you live in a part of the world where earthquakes are likely to happen, you need to have a plan ahead of time. Fasten tall furniture to the wall so it won't fall over. Then choose a safe place in every room of your house and school. If you hide under a sturdy table or desk, nothing can fall on your head.

Then practice DROP, COVER, AND HOLD ON! Drop under something sturdy, hold on to something, and hide your eyes by pressing your arm against your face.

Have a disaster kit ready. The kit should have first-aid supplies (like medicine and bandages). It should also have canned food and a can opener, bottled water, a battery-operated radio, a flashlight, clothing that will protect you from cold and water, and written instructions on how to turn off electricity, gas, and water.

Then, if an earthquake happens, DROP, COVER, AND HOLD ON! Stay indoors until the shaking stops. Stay away from windows. If you're outdoors, find a spot away from buildings, trees, and power lines—and drop to the ground. If you're in a car, tell the driver to slow down and drive to a safe place. Stay in the car until the shaking stops.

Once the shaking stops, check to see if anyone is hurt. Help the adults see if the building is hurt. Make sure there's nothing that could cause a fire. Turn off electricity and gas lines. Be ready for the smaller shocks that come after a big earthquake. Each time you feel one, DROP, COVER, AND HOLD ON!

## VOLCANOES

If you live near a volcano that might erupt, make a plan ahead of time. Make a disaster kit, like the one we talked about under "Earthquakes."

Make sure your family knows the best route to get away from the volcano.

Then if the volcano erupts, follow instructions. Try not to be anywhere that the wind could blow hot ash on you. If you're inside, close the windows. Bring any animals you have inside too. If you're outside, go inside! If you can't, roll up in a ball and protect your head. Don't stay near streams of water, because the water can carry burning stuff from the volcano. Move to higher ground because the hot stuff from the volcano will flow downhill.

After the volcano, when you go outside, wear long-sleeve shirts and long pants to protect your skin from ash. Wear goggles to protect your eyes. Wear a dust mask so you don't breathe in the ash. Grown-ups will need to get the ash off buildings. The ash is very heavy, so it could make the building fall down.

## TSUNAMIS

If you live near a coast where a tsunami might hit, make a plan ahead of time. Your family should know the best route to get away from danger. Make a disaster kit for your home and car. The kit should contain all the things listed under "Earthquakes." If you hear that a tsunami is coming, follow any instructions you are given. Get to higher ground and go as far away from the water as you can.

After the tsunami, grown-ups will need to help people who are hurt or trapped. Stay out of a building if there is water around it. The water could make the building fall down. Be very careful when you go back to your house. Check for anything that could cause a fire. Open windows and doors so things can dry out.

Our planet is an amazing place. There's a lot going on inside it. Sometimes, it can really shake us up!

The more you can learn about the Earth, the more you'll understand. Learning gives you power. Things like earthquakes, volcanoes, and tsunamis won't seem quite so scary. You'll know there are ways you, your family, and your friends can stay safe!

# Find Out More

**ONLINE**
These sites will tell you more about earthquakes, volcanoes, and tsunamis. On some of the sites, you can watch videos.

Ancient Wave of Poseidon
www.livescience.com/19809-ancient-wave-real-tsunami.html

Discovery Kids: What Causes Earthquakes?
kids.discovery.com/tell-me/curiosity-corner/earth/natural-disasters/
   how-earthquakes-work

Do Something: Tsunamis
www.dosomething.org/tipsandtools/11-facts-about-tsunamis

National Geographic: Earthquakes
video.nationalgeographic.com/video/environment/
   environment-natural-disasters/earthquakes/earthquake-101

National Geographic: Volcanoes
video.nationalgeographic.com/video/kids/forces-of-nature-kids/
   volcanoes-101-kids

Science Kids: What Is an Earthquake?
www.sciencekids.co.nz/videos/earth/whatisanearthquake.html

NOAA: Tsunami Information for Kids
www.tsunami.noaa.gov/kids.html

U.S. Geological Survey: Earthquakes for Kids
earthquake.usgs.gov/learn/kids

Volcano World
volcano.oregonstate.edu/kids

Waves of Destruction: History's Biggest Tsunamis
www.livescience.com/19618-history-biggest-tsunamis.html

Weather WizKids: Earthquakes
www.weatherwizkids.com/weather-earthquake.htm

**FIND OUT MORE IN BOOKS**

*Here are some books we recommend if you want to learn more. See if you can find some of them in your library.*

Editors of Time. *Time for Kids: Earthquakes!* New York: Harper Collins, 2006.

Editors of Time. *Time for Kids: Volcanoes!* New York: Harper Collins, 2006.

Furgang, Kathy. *National Geographic Kids: Everything Volcanoes and Earthquakes.* Washington, D.C.: National Geographic Books, 2013

Ganeri, Anita. *Eruption! The Story of Volcanoes.* New York: Penguin, 2012.

KidCaps. *The Science of Tsunamis.* Seattle, Washington: CreateSpace, 2013.

Schreiber, Anne. *Volcanoes!* Washington, D.C.: National Geographic Books, 2011.

# Glossary Words

When you are reading websites and other books, you may run into words you don't know. Here are some words that have to do with earthquakes, volcanoes, and tsunamis. These words weren't used in this book, but you may run across them in other books and websites.

**Aftershocks**: The smaller quakes that happen after a big earthquake.

**Crater**: A steep, circle-shaped hollow that sometimes forms after a volcano.

**Dormant**: A dormant volcano is one that is sleeping. It isn't shooting out lava or ash. But it could wake up!

**Evacuate**: When people are moved out of an area before a natural disaster hits.

**Fault**: A crack in the Earth's crust. Faults are usually found along the edges of the tectonic plates. They're where earthquakes and volcanoes happen most often.

**Geysers**: Boiling water that shoots out of the Earth, high into the air. They are caused by the heat from volcanoes heating up water beneath the ground.

**Magnitude**: The strength of an earthquake. Scientists measure the magnitude of earthquakes with numbers from the Richter Scale.

**Richter Scale**: Numbers used to measure how strong earthquakes are. Most earthquakes that happen are lower than a 3 on the Richter Scale. People don't usually even feel them. Earthquakes over 7 are considered dangerous. The highest earthquake ever measured was 9.5. It was in Chile in 1960.

**Seismic**: Having to do with the waves that move through the Earth. A seismograph is an instrument that shows how big earthquake waves are by writing on a roll of specially marked graph paper. A seismologist is a scientist who studies earthquakes.

**Vent**: An opening in the Earth where magma, ash, and gas can shoot out.

# Index

An index is a quick way to look inside a book for a certain thing. It helps you find what you're looking for by giving you all the page numbers where you'll read that word.

ash 22, 27, 35, 41
atmosphere 23

Chile 39
core 19, 23
crust 10–11, 16, 18, 20–21

disaster kit 40–41

earthquake 7, 10–12, 16–21, 23–26, 28–29, 31–42
engineers 39
epicenter 16

Haiti 33

Indian Ocean 36

Japan 31, 37

Kashmir 32

lava 8–9, 20–22, 27, 34–35
Lisbon 28

magma 8, 14, 20–21, 34
Mount Etna 26–27
Mount Merapi 35, 38
Mount St. Helens 34
Mount Vesuvius 27
mountain 8–9, 18–21, 23, 35

ocean 12, 24, 31, 33, 36

Pacific Ocean 31
Pompeii 27
Poseidon 30

rain 18

river 19

San Francisco 39
scientists 17, 19, 30–31, 35, 38
Shaanxi 28

tectonic plate 14, 17, 20
tsunami 7, 12–14, 24, 26, 28, 30–31, 36–38, 40–42

volcano 7–9, 12, 14, 20–27, 34–35, 38, 40–42
Vulcan 26

wave 12, 16, 25, 30–31, 36
weather 18

# About the Author

Chance Parker is a teacher and a writer. He has felt a couple of very small earthquakes, but he has never been in a big one. A few years ago, though, he traveled to the island of Montserrat, where a big volcano has been blowing its top for several years. The volcano has taken away homes and businesses. Chance was able to see the big rocks that have landed in people's yards, thrown there by the volcano. He talked to children who have grown up with a volcano in their backyard! In 2005, Chance also traveled to Thailand, where he talked to people who had lived through the big tsunami there. He saw the places where the tsunami had swept away buildings. In one place, the only thing left from a family's home was the toilet! Chance talked to a man who ended up sitting in a tree after the tsunami, waiting for someone to come and help him get down. All those things have made Chance Parker very interested in volcanoes, earthquakes, and tsunamis.

# Picture Credits

p. 7: Fotolia: © Denis Tabler, © Art3D
p. 8: Fotolia: © Andrea Danti, © Slimsepp, © Art3D
p. 9: Fotolia: © Glucchesi, © JCraft5, © IDuarte
p. 10: Fotolia: © Pavelis, © Eagle
p. 11: Fotolia: © FiCo74, © Tom Wang, © Mopic
p. 12: © Designua | Dreamstime.com
p. 13: Fotolia: © IgOrZh, © View Apart
p. 14: Village Earth Press; Fotolia: © Art3D
p. 15: Village Earth Press; © Picsfive | Dreamstime.com, Fotolia: © Art3D
p. 16: Village Earth Press; Fotolia: © Kubals,
p. 17: Village Earth Press
p. 18: © Cory Thoman | Dreamstime.com; Fotolia: © Anton Sokolov; © Merkushev | Dreamstime.com
p. 19: Fotolia: © Doan Oakenheim, © Greg Pickens, © Art3D; © Madartists | Dreamstime.com
p. 20: Fotolia: © Maximo Sanz
p. 21: Fotolias: © Sunshine Pics; © Designua | Dreamstime.com
p. 22: Fotolia: © Nlyazz; © Art3D; © Blagov58 | Dreamstime.com; © Peter Emmett | Dreamstime.com
p. 23: Fotolia: © Byelikova Oksana, © Art3D; © Selestron76 | Dreamstime.com
p. 24: Village Earth Press
p. 25: Paul Topp | Dreamstime.com; U.S. National Park Service
p. 26: Fotolia: © Malchev, © Art3D
p. 27: Fotolia: © AM Design, © Frenta, © Art3D
p. 28: public domain
p. 29: U.S. Library of Congress
p. 30: Walter Crane
p. 31: Katsushika Hokusai
p. 32: U.S. Navy
p. 33: United Nations; U.S. Navy
p. 34: U.S. Geological Survey
p. 35: Bert Lanting; NASA; Fotolia: © Art3D
p. 36: NASA; Fotolia: © Art3D
p. 37: Fotolia: © Paolo74
p. 38: © Akbar Solo | Dreamstime.com
p. 39: Fotolia: © Rafael Ramirez, © Art3D; U.S. Geological Survey
p. 42: Fololia: © Michael Jung

www.ingramcontent.com/pod-product-compliance
Lightning Source LLC
Chambersburg PA
CBHW061358090426

42743CB00002B/65